# HOW TO GET WHAT YOU WANT BY HELPING ENOUGH OTHER PEOPLE GET WHAT THEY WANT

## AND 4 OTHER SALES SECRETS YOU MAY NOT KNOW ABOUT

BY

## T.J. ROHLEDER

### THE BLUE JEANS MILLIONAIRE

# TABLE OF CONTENTS

# INTRODUCTION

## How to get what you want by helping enough other people get what they want.

———————— ⁊ை⥁ ————————

Getting into sales and marketing completely transformed my life. It gave me a level of confidence I never had before, and I can now talk to anyone about anything. I enjoy the creative side of sales—it's an artistic way to make money. I love getting paid based on results, not just my time, which puts me in the same league as some of the wealthiest people. Knowing that my future is in my own hands, and I have control over it, is incredibly empowering.

**Learning to sell has impacted every part of my life.** It's helped me build my own business, and led to many exciting and lucrative opportunities. Sure, there were challenges, but each one made me smarter and better at what I do. Over time, I've built automated marketing systems that let me reach millions of people, and I've mastered the art and science of sales. My obsession with the best, most effective sales strategies has been thrilling.

The most exciting part? **I've figured out how the average person with no sales experience can stay home and make more money in just a few hours a day than most people make working full-time.** This is the breakthrough I want to share with others!

## My mission is to help as many people as possible change their lives by teaching them my proven methods.

I want to train thousands of new salespeople and help others who are struggling in sales or barely getting by. I have the solution that will allow them to earn more with less effort, all while having more fun. It all starts with this little book...

This little book contains six of my greatest secrets, all drawn and expanded on from my 139-page book called, *No-Pressure Sales System.*

The first secret is what I call **ethical manipulation.** That's why I titled this book *How to Get Everything You Want by Helping Other People Get What They Want.* In the world of selling, it's crucial to understand that...

## Success comes from helping others achieve their goals.

Ethical manipulation means creating win-win situations where you get what you want by genuinely helping others get what they wand and need.

This concept is just the beginning. As you'll see, along with the topic of ethical manipulation, this book contains five Chapters, each one covering an additional secret. If you find these ideas valuable, I invite you to get my full *No-Pressure Sales System* book, which contains all 144 of my proven tips, tricks, and strategies.

As a bonus, I'll also include...

**A free 30-minute consultation and let me personally help you apply these methods to maximize your success.**

If you're looking to make more money and change your life, what you're about to discover can do just that. Sales can completely transform your life, just like it did mine!

Will this small book actually change your life?

The answer will surprise you!

Aristotle Onassis once said...

**"The secret to getting rich is to know something that nobody else knows."**

This quote perfectly applies to this small book, because I've learned some things about making money that very few people know. With a lot of help and support from my wife Eileen, I went from $300 to nearly $10 million in our first five years of business. We never looked back. In this small book, I'll share just a few of those little-known ideas. I've got lots more!

What's even better is that I'll show you how to make money in the tough, high-pressure sales industry ... but without using high-pressure tactics. You're gonna love this!

With over 40 years in sales, I've developed methods that are low-pressure and simple. And guess what? They work like magic! The proof? It's in the millions of dollars in transactions that we and others who know these secrets have experienced. I've worked hard to master the art of making money, and I've done it without resorting to high-pressure sales tactics.

I genuinely enjoy sharing my best insights and helping people achieve success. That's one of my biggest strengths. Over the years, I've learned how to turn small amounts of money into substantial fortunes, and I'm passionate about passing that knowledge on to others.

My Clients, Members, and Affiliates – and even folks considering coming on board can all sense this about me. It's one of the reasons people say they trust me and want me to help them. Of course, there's more to my success than simply getting help from someone who cares. While being kind and supportive is important, what sets me apart is combining that with proven strategies for creating massive wealth. If you can bring a little self-motivation and drive to succeed, then I can give you the secrets you need to get the results you want.

That's what makes me different. And it's what you'll learn from me. The methods and strategies I share aren't like anything you've seen before. I guarantee it!

Take your time reading this book. Don't let its size fool you—inside are powerful tips, tricks, and strategies that I use to generate extraordinary results for myself, my Members and Affiliates, and other coaching Clients I work with. It's all here for you to learn and apply.

## My Special Offer to You.

This book contains six out of 144 total secrets from my **No-Pressure Sales System** book. These ideas are completely different from anything you'll find in typical "best selling" sales books. I know this because I've read an entire library of them. Most of those sales books only have one or two good ideas.

My **No-Pressure Sales System** book is jam-packed with **144 secrets**. Six of those secrets are included in this small book. Toward the back of this small book, I'll give you a list of some of these secrets, so watch for that.

Take some time to go over these tips, tricks, and strategies. If you find them helpful—and I know you will—fill out the Form in the back. When you do, I'll rush you a copy of my **No-Pressure Sales System** book with all 144 of my proven methods.

Place your order today, and I'll also include a **free 30-minute private coaching session** so I can personally show you how to start making more money with these strategies.

Dive into this book. Turn to the back and fill out the Form. And take action today to get the full book with all 144 secrets. You'll be glad you did!

In the meantime, I hope you enjoy this short book.

Sincerely,

T.J. Rohleder
The Blue Jeans Millionaire
Call Me! 620-869-7074

# SECRET #1

## How to <u>ethically</u> become a master manipulator and make tons of money.

———— ✾ ————

S elling can be tough, but if you want to succeed, you need to face one brutal truth:

### All selling is manipulation.

At first, I didn't want to accept this. Manipulation is a negative word. Most people don't like it. The word "manipulation" makes us think of someone being dishonest. Like someone trying to deceive others to only get what they want. We certainly don't want to be that person.

But the truth is that selling is about the fine art of persuading someone to part with their money to get something they want and/or need. And that's manipulation in its simplest form.

Here's the thing: Buyers typically do everything they can to hold onto their money, even when buying something helps them achieve their wants, needs, or goals. As a seller, your job is to help convince them that it's in their best interest to give it to you. It's a back-and-forth—like a tug-of-war. You have to get good at playing the role they need you to play. You must become who they need you to be in order to help them see the value in what you offer.

In this sense, manipulation doesn't have to be a bad word. The key is to offer value. Good, honest salespeople aren't trying to rip people off or cheat them. That's a silly game with bad outcomes. No, a good salesperson is attempting to prove beyond any shadow of a doubt that what they offer is worth far more to their prospective customer than the money they are being asked to give up. It's a value exchange. Their money for your offer.

**When you deliver real value, you're using manipulation in a positive way. You can feel good about what you do. And because of this, you'll build a loyal customer base who keeps coming back for more.**

The best way to think about sales manipulation is this Zig Ziglar quote:

## "You can get what you want by helping enough other people get what they want."

I first learned this idea when I got involved in network marketing. I came across this quote and it really stuck with me over the years. Listen to it in your own head as you read it one more time: **"You can have anything in life you want if you'll help enough other people get what they want."** I loved that message. It made sense to me. And it changed my way of thinking about the art of selling.

Selling, in its essence, is manipulation. People always try to hold on to their money. And as the seller, your job is to influence them to give it to you. But manipulation isn't always negative. It depends on your intentions.

## Striving to get your way is natural.

Let me give you an example. When I was a kid, my mom ruled the house. My dad was often away on business. So when we kids wanted something, we'd go to our dad first.

He'd always tell us, "Go ask your mom." The inference was that if mom's good with it, then I'm good, too. So, we'd run to mom and say something like, "Dad said it's okay." That wasn't exactly what he said, but we were trying to influence her decision.

We were manipulating—and it worked!

Manipulation is natural. Every kid knows how to do it. Every spouse knows how to do it. We all do it! In fact, we're hardwired to do it. It's in our DNA...

Some of my first experiences with selling happened when I was a teenager. Back in the 1970s, when marijuana was illegal everywhere, I used to sell it. I'm not proud of it. And I'm not advocating drug use. Please understand me. I worked hard to get and stay sober, and I've been completely clean for over 40 years now.

But back in the 1970s, I was young, rebellious, and I didn't know any better. I'm sharing this story because it's part of my journey, and it connects to the idea of "getting what you want by helping others get what they want."

Here's how it worked: I would buy quarter-pound of marijuana and sell just three ounces. Every time. By selling 3/4ths of my supply, I got to keep the 4th ounce for free. My motto back then was simple:

### 'Sell three, get mine for free!"

Over a couple of years, I started purchasing "kilos" and dividing them up, "helping others get what they want, so I could get what I wanted."

For me...

## Selling was <u>always</u> about offering value and receiving something I wanted in return.

So when I first discovered network marketing in the 1980s, it clicked. I loved it because it allowed me to offer value to others while getting what I wanted in return. I realized that the best way to sell is to show people that what you have is worth far more than the money you're asking for.

That's how you can create lasting relationships and build a successful business—by helping others get what they want. It's win/win!

Stop thinking of manipulation as something bad. Manipulation can actually be a powerful and positive thing—it all comes down to your intentions.

What are you truly trying to do? Are you trying to help people? Are you offering real value? Are you focused on something positive and worthwhile? Does what you offer actually deliver on its promises? And are you targeting the right people with your sales message?

If your answers to all these questions are "yes," then embrace the fact that you are a manipulator—and be proud of it. Great salespeople learn how to become master manipulators. The more you accept this idea, the more successful you will become.

If you're genuinely trying to help people and offer something of true value, and you're working with the right people, you can make significant amounts of money by helping people get what they want.

# SECRET #2

## Selling is a Game You Play to Win!

⸺⸲⸲⸲⸺

Selling is the ultimate game, because you control the money you can make. It's about understanding people. What they fear, what they hope for, and what they secretly desire. You use that knowledge to create sales messages that speak directly to their hearts.

I didn't always see sales as a game. In the beginning, I just wanted a way to make more money. I hated working in factories and doing physical labor. I saw sales as a way out and a way to make money. Many people get into sales for the same reason, but years later, I realized sales is more than just a job. It's an adventure. If you start seeing it that way, you'll have more fun and make more money.

### "You can write your own paycheck!"

In the fall of 2016, my brother-in-law, Jim, asked me to speak to a group of troubled students at a continuation school. Jim is a guidance counselor who helps kids recognize their strengths and overcome their problems. When I was their age, I was one of those kids. I dropped out of High School three different times. Imagine that! I hated school. I was rebellious and on drugs. I didn't think I had a future.

Jim said I could reach these kids in a positive way, so I shared my story with them.

I told them about how I was just like them in school—doing drugs, selling drugs, failing at school. But I also told them about how I found a way out through sales. I didn't just work for a paycheck—**I learned to write my own paycheck.**

That's when the kids really started to pay attention. That excited them.

These kids didn't care much about my story until I said those magic words: **"I got into sales to write my own paycheck!"** That caught their attention! At first, I think they thought I was talking about doing something illegal, like counterfeiting money. But of course, what I meant was that when you're in sales, you control how much you earn. It's not about how much time you put in—it's about the results you deliver. **Some salespeople even make more than the CEOs of their companies.**

Sales is the lifeblood of any business, and the best entrepreneurs are the best salespeople. When you learn the art and science of sales, you can make massive amounts of money. The key is to understand what people want and give it to them. If you're willing to put in the work and surround yourself with the right people and opportunities, you can become a millionaire.

The students didn't understand what I meant at first, but by the end of my speech, they saw that sales isn't just about a job—it's about taking control of your future and making your own rules.

## Living on a fixed income is like being in prison.

That's how I felt when I was working in a factory, getting paid by the hour. I was a welder, but I wasn't skilled enough to make a lot of money. I didn't realize then that sales was the key to escaping that prison. I didn't see selling as something I could enjoy, nor did I understand how much money I could make from it.

But then I found sales, and the pursuit of sales excellence completely changed my life!

As I eventually learned...

---

## Sales is an incredible game!

It's about understanding people on a deep emotional level— knowing why they buy certain products and services. When you truly understand their needs, you can show them that what you're offering is worth far more than the money they'll give up in exchange. The goal is to make them feel that what they're getting from you is so valuable that parting with their money seems insignificant.

---

Developing great marketing systems is the key to turning prospects into loyal customers, and keeping them coming back for more. The best marketing systems automate the entire selling process, making it easy to bring in money without pressure. It's about creating a system where people are practically begging you to take their money.

Selling is about understanding what people want and giving it to them in a way that makes them happy to pay for it. It's a game of knowing your customers better than they know themselves. And once you see selling as the great adventure it is, you'll realize just how exciting—and profitable—it can be.

**For example, one of the things I love to do—and what I'm going to teach you -- is how to create marketing systems that sell.** This can be both enjoyable and highly profitable once you figure it out.

## Building marketing systems is like playing an exciting game where you aim to win!

A marketing system is like a money machine. How would you like to own your own money machine? Of course you would! **Everybody would love to have a money machine they could turn on whenever they need more money. That's exactly what a good sales and marketing system does.** I'll teach you how to develop a system like this—something most salespeople don't know how to create. But you will, once you go through our coaching program and get the help, support, and guidance we offer.

Being a professional sales and marketing expert means living an unconventional life. You're not working for a job or just earning a paycheck.

Sales is like a game, and like all games, it has very specific rules. There are many skills and strategies involved, and when you know them, you can win every day. You know exactly what you need to do to succeed, how much money you want to make, and what your goals are. And each time you make a sale, you'll feel that rush of success—endorphins will flood your brain, and you'll feel amazing.

Can you get that feeling from a regular job? No way!

Sales is the ultimate game because, every day, you have clear objectives, and the more sales you make, the more money you earn. It's about upselling, cross-selling, and repeat business. **With sales, you're always improving your knowledge and skills, and as you get better, you make more money. That's exciting!** It's something you can't get in a regular job. In sales, you're paid for your performance—you're rewarded for the results you bring in.

It's like a great sporting event every single day. And as you contribute to your company and your family, you'll feel great because your work makes a difference. Every company needs more sales and profits, and in sales, you're the hero. **That's why selling is the greatest game on earth!**

### Every day, the question isn't,
### "Am I going to make money?"
### but "How much money
### am I going to make?"

I wake up every morning and can't wait to discover the answer to that question! The goal is to get more people to give you money, more often, and for more profit. It's about bigger sales, repeat business, and building strong relationships with your customers. It's also about getting referrals and developing systems that make the process easier. You can spend your whole life mastering these skills, and the better you get, the more money you can earn. Striving for greatness is a key part of playing the sales game.

But wait, there's more! Selling is a **much deeper game** than you think. For instance...

> **The best thing I love about sales is teaching others how to play the game. There's nothing more satisfying than being part of a sales team, all working together to make money and have fun! It's not just a job or a career; it becomes part of who you are. It's like any other team sport: Every day, you're striving to get better at it.**

One more quick story: I live in Kansas, surrounded by farmers. Farmers don't punch time clocks. For them, farming isn't a job—it's a way of life. The same is true for great salespeople and entrepreneurs. Selling isn't just something you do; it's part of who you are. That's the mindset you need to succeed in sales.

The better you get at sales, the more money you can make. And the more money you make, the more motivated you become. Sales, like any great game, can be complicated and challenging, but that's what makes it exciting. The better your competition, the better you have to be. That's why I got back into network marketing—to compete and push myself to be the best. Sales is the ultimate game, and it's a sport that rewards you for your efforts.

# SECRET #3

## The true reason why someone will buy whatever you sell.

❦

I n 1984, I learned a lesson about sales hat changed my life. I was just getting started in the world of selling, and someone shared a principle with me that, at the time, seemed almost too simple to believe. They told me,

**"Selling is an emotional experience.**

**People buy for emotional reasons and**

**then justify their purchase logically."**

At first, I didn't believe it. I thought, "That can't be true. People buy for all kinds of reasons, and surely logic has to play a bigger role." But as I gained more experience, I realized just how powerful that principle is. Decades later, it remains the foundation of everything I do in sales.

### People don't want to admit that they buy for emotional reasons.

Most people like to believe they are completely logical and rational. But the reality is, emotions are at the heart of every decision, especially when it comes to buying. People want to feel good about themselves or feel better about their situation, and they use logic to justify those emotional choices that they make.

Let me share a story to prove this. As someone who sells business opportunities, particularly in the network marketing industry, you might think the main reason people are drawn to these opportunities is to make money. On the surface, that seems true. But when you dig deeper, it's not just about the money.

What people really want is how the money will make them feel. They imagine the freedom it will give them, the pride they'll feel in achieving something big, or the security they'll create for their family. It's not the dollars in their bank account they're chasing—it's the emotions tied to what those dollars represent.

This is why understanding the emotional side of sales is so important. If you can connect with people on an emotional level and show them how your product or opportunity will make their lives better, they'll justify the decision with logic. And they'll feel great about it.

The most successful salespeople in history understood this. They knew that every purchase comes down to an emotional desire to feel good or improve one's situation. Once you grasp this principle and learn how to use it, you'll unlock a new level of success in whatever you're selling.

Now that we're on the subject of emotions...

## Here's how I became emotionally tied to the business opportunity market.

In my 20s, I hated my life. I was working as a welder in a factory, building mobile home frames. The work was hot, dirty, and exhausting, but it was the only skill I had. I felt stuck, miserable, and completely hopeless. Before that, I had struggled in school, barely scraping by, and I didn't have any big plans for my future.

Then everything changed. I discovered the network marketing industry, and for the first time, I saw a way out. It gave me hope. I became obsessed—not with money itself, but with what money could represent: freedom, purpose, and a chance to build something meaningful. It was an emotional turning point for me, and it inspired me to believe that maybe I could do something great with my life.

That obsession drove me to learn everything I could about sales, marketing, and business opportunities. I realized that I wasn't just chasing money—I was chasing the chance to feel good about myself and radically improve my life. And I wasn't alone. I discovered that everyone getting involved in business opportunities is looking for the same thing: a way to feel better about themselves, improve their circumstances, and never worry about money again.

This insight became my secret weapon.

People buy for emotional reasons, even if they justify their decisions logically. Once I understood this, everything clicked. My wife and I went on to build a business that made millions of dollars. She ran the operations brilliantly, while I focused on sales and marketing by telling my story.

Why did that work? Because <u>my</u> <u>story</u> <u>was</u> <u>their</u> <u>story</u>. I knew what it felt like to be stuck, frustrated, and desperate for a way out. I understood their struggles because I had lived them. The more I shared my journey—the setbacks, the scams, and the moments of hope—the more people connected with me. They saw themselves in my story, and that connection was powerful.

21

**If I could only give one piece of advice, it's this: Find a market you truly understand on an intimate level. For me, it was getting into <u>the business</u> <u>opportunity</u> <u>world</u> because I had lived it. I knew the pain, the desire, and the drive people had to change their lives. That understanding was what made all the difference.**

If you can connect with people emotionally and show them how your opportunity can help them feel better, they'll trust you. Then, give them logical reasons to justify their decision, and they'll be ready to take action. That's the heart of sales, and it's how you can build something meaningful for yourself and others.

## The emotional reasons someone buys a business opportunity.

People get involved in network marketing and business opportunities because they are searching for something more. They aren't happy with their current lives, and they're often worried about their future. These are deep emotional drivers—worry, fear, and a desire for growth. They have dreams they want to fulfill. They feel stuck and are looking for a better way.

This unhappiness and desire for something greater are what push people to take action. It's not just about the product or opportunity; it's about their hope for a brighter future. People buy for emotional reasons, even if they later justify their decisions with logic. That's why the opportunities and products you offer must be solid and credible.

One opportunity I'm involved with right now is silver and gold investing. It's incredibly powerful because silver and gold have always maintained their value. This makes it easy for people to justify their decision logically while also feeling secure emotionally.

When you understand that people buy emotionally, you can focus on their biggest fears, desires, and dreams. Sometimes they can't even put those feelings into words, but they know deep down that they want more. They want the dream to feel real. They're looking for a way out of pain and a path toward something better.

## This is why stories are so powerful.

People identify with stories of others who wanted to change their lives, who had dreams, and who made those dreams come true. These emotional connections are the real reasons why people get involved in business opportunities and the network marketing industry.

But there's even more to it. Network marketing and affiliate opportunities allow people to succeed by helping others succeed. That's pure emotion—it's about more than just making money. It's about improving your own life by helping others improve theirs.

When I first got involved in the network marketing world, that emotional element hit me hard. I loved the idea that I could make my life better by helping others do the same. I didn't just want to earn money—I wanted to make a difference in people's lives. That desire to help others while succeeding myself is one of the most powerful motivators I've ever felt.

This is why network marketing, affiliate programs, and business opportunities are so exciting! They're not just about money. They're about helping families, feeling good about yourself, and making a real impact. People want to improve their lives while helping others do the same, and that's what makes these kinds of opportunities so emotionally compelling.

# SECRET #4

## Albert Einstein's greatest secret that makes you a ton of money.

―――――― ೫ᐧᑲ᠍ᢀ ――――――

C reating a great sales message takes time, effort, and a lot of thought. It's not something that happens overnight. The best ideas come after brainstorming, testing, and rethinking. Sales and marketing is something you can learn the basics in a day or two, but mastering them takes a lifetime. I love that idea because it's so true.

What's the secret to mastering sales and marketing?

Albert Einstein said it best:

### "Genius is one percent inspiration and 99 percent perspiration."

That couldn't be more accurate when it comes to sales and marketing. The more you learn and the longer you stick with it, the more successful you can become. The good news is, there are shortcuts and secrets. That's exactly what I aim to share with you in this book and through the coaching programs we offer.

These are the ideas that have made me millions of dollars. And here's the truth: there's nothing special about me. I just got obsessed with figuring out what it takes to succeed in sales, marketing, and business. In fact...

## Discovering sales and marketing changed the course of my life forever.

When I was in my early 20s, my life wasn't going anywhere. I hated school and wasn't interested in college. I was stuck. Then, I discovered the exciting world of network marketing. I started joining different opportunities, which eventually led me to discover direct response marketing.

In December 1985, I launched my first business with a small carpet and upholstery cleaning service. That was the start of it all. **I became deeply committed to learning everything I could about how to turn small amounts of money into a fortune.**

When I met my wife Eileen, she saw how many "get rich quick" programs I had bought. Many of these programs focused on direct response marketing—a system that's more about selling than traditional advertising. It's about getting enough people to pay you enough money over a long enough time to create real success.

## This led me to the ultimate formula for business success.

**It's simple, but incredibly powerful. Here's the five-step formula:**

1. Get enough people.
2. To pay you enough money.
3. Enough times.

4. With a large enough profit per transaction.

5. And you can do all of this with maximum efficiency.

Mastering these five things can help you turn small amounts of money into big fortunes. That's what I did. I started with just $300 and a lot of determination. With the help of my amazing wife, Eileen (who ran our business for 12 years), I turned that small startup into millions.

## If I can do it, so can you.

There's nothing magical about my story—it's about learning, persistence, and applying proven strategies. With the right tools and mindset, you can achieve the same kind of success in your own life.

Albert Einstein admitted that his secret to success was that he was "constantly groping." At first, I misunderstood what he meant by "groping." I only associated it with the silly things teenagers might do. But later, I realized what he really meant: it's about reaching, striving, and asking yourself the right questions.

It's about constantly asking, "How can I do better?" How can you get enough people—of the right kind—to pay you enough money, over and over again, to create success? How can you truly understand what people want and deliver it in a way that nobody else can?

To do this, you need to deeply understand your audience. People buy for emotional reasons, often unconscious ones. Your job is to figure out who they are, what motivates them, and how to reach them with messages that resonate. **When you understand their desires better than they do, you can create products and services that**

**make them excited and eager to buy.** This small book is my way of sharing these ideas with you. It's a glimpse into the best strategies I've learned from marketing masters like Russ von Hoelscher, Dan Kennedy, and Gary Halbert. These were the people who helped me understand how to turn small sums of money into massive fortunes.

They had already solved the problems I was trying to figure out. They taught me the methods, the mindset, and the strategies to achieve success, and now I'm passing those lessons on to you. Through programs like the *Get More Customers Association*, *Direct Mail Mastery*, and the *No Pressure Sales System*, we teach step-by-step how to do what I learned from these masters. This book is just a taste of the best of what I've discovered. My goal is to inspire you to take action, learn more, and let us help you the same way others helped me.

This is also what you need to do with your own buyers. Show them a taste of what's possible, inspire them, and help them see the value you offer. When you connect with people on an emotional level and show them how you can solve their problems, they'll want to work with you.

Success starts with understanding your audience, creating products they truly need, and delivering those products with messages that excite and inspire them. If you master this, you'll be well on your way to achieving greatness.

## Sales and marketing give you the power to make money and grow any business.

Imagine this: how do you get the most people to give you the most money, as often as possible, for the longest period of time? How do you maximize your profit per transaction? How do you create sales messages that get people so excited they can't wait to buy what you're offering? How do you build automated systems that work like a money machine? What would that look like?

These are the questions that captivate my imagination every single day. They get me out of bed in the morning, and they can inspire you too. Selling is a game where every day is an exciting challenge, and you always know if you're winning by the results you're seeing—the money you're making and the impact you're having.

Albert Einstein was so engrossed in his work that there are stories of him walking down the street in his underwear because he forgot to put on pants! That kind of **deep obsession** is what drives the best scientists—and it's also what drives the best sales and marketing professionals.

**The simple five-step formula I shared earlier is the key to business success. It works for businesses of all sizes and industries. Here's another way to look at it:**

- Attract enough people for whatever you sell.
- Make sure they're the right kind of people.
- Create offers that get them to pay you enough money with each transaction.
- Then get them to buy more often.
- And maximize your efficiency in everything you do. Try to avoid wasted energy and resources.

Your job is to master this formula. Create sales messages that excite people! Make them eager to do business with you! Understand your competitors and why they're succeeding, so you can learn from them while setting yourself apart. It's all about getting people excited, stimulating their thinking, and building relationships that lead to more business over time.

## This isn't just work—it's a game, and it's one of the most exciting games you'll ever play.

The secret to winning lies in what Einstein said: deep commitment and hard work. You have to wake up every morning and decide that you're going to be the best at what you do.

That's my story. I became obsessed with mastering sales and marketing. I wanted to be the best I could be, and I was inspired by the people I worked with along the way. My goal is to inspire you in the same way. When you join one of our coaching programs or get involved with the opportunities we promote, I'll help you become the best you can be too.

This small booklet is just the beginning. I can only teach you so much here, but my hope

is to spark your imagination and get you so excited that you'll naturally want to learn more. The more you learn, the more you can earn.

Now, let's move on to the next strategy!

# SECRET #5

## The biggest thing we sell, but it's missing from every sales book.

———— ⧉ ————

When it comes to sales and marketing, one thing matters most: results.

**People buy products and services to solve their problems—whether real or perceived. Your success comes from understanding those problems and offering the right solutions.** At the heart of it, people are looking for emotional outcomes. <u>This</u> <u>is</u> <u>something</u> <u>most</u> <u>sales</u> <u>books</u> <u>overlook</u>. The better you understand what people truly want, the easier it is to offer solutions they can't resist. I'll show you exactly how to do this.

I've spent years asking myself one question: What are people really searching for, and how can I give it to them? This question has shaped everything I do in business. People don't just want a product or service—they want the emotional benefit it provides. They want to feel secure, happy, successful, and free.

One of the first lessons in sales is **the difference between features and benefits.** Features are what a product or service *is* or *does*. Benefits, on the other hand, are the emotional results people achieve when they buy it. Here's the best definition I've ever found:

## A benefit is <u>the</u> <u>emotional</u> <u>result</u> a prospective customer or client can experience after they buy your product or service.

That's what people really care about—the transformation it creates in their lives.

When I first discovered this, it completely changed the way I approached business.

Back in 1988, I was stuck in a job I hated with no way out. I didn't have any special skills or experience, but I knew I wanted something different. That's when I found network marketing. For the first time, I learned about leverage—the idea of earning income through the efforts of others, not just my own time and energy.

This concept changed everything for me. Instead of working one hour to earn one hour of pay, I could earn through systems and teams. It wasn't easy at first, but it was life-changing. I discovered that by offering people opportunities and solutions, I could help them change their lives too.

Since then, I've made it my mission to share these ideas with others. I know what it's like to feel stuck and hopeless, and I know how empowering it is to find a way out. Selling isn't about pushing products—it's about helping people achieve the results they're looking for. And when you focus on delivering real benefits, success follows naturally.

If you can master this, you can change lives— including your own.

### How we quickly made our first million.

Back in the 1980s, my wife and I launched our first promotion called "**Dialing for Dollars**." It was a way to use

31

a simple answering machine—a new technology at the time—to make money without having to talk to anyone. Answering machines were just becoming popular and affordable, and people were curious about how to use them creatively. We saw an opportunity to solve a problem and turned it into something that people loved.

The concept was simple: use an answering machine to handle part of the sales process automatically. Instead of a salesperson having to call and explain everything, the answering machine did the work for you. It was a new idea at the time, and it worked incredibly well. The key to its success was a headline written by my mentor, Russ Von Hoelscher that said something like:

*"$843 a day receiving phone calls—and you never have to talk to anyone!"*

That headline grabbed people's attention. It made them curious. It made them want to know more, and they couldn't resist reading the rest of the sales message. **Over the next five years, that idea brought in over 160,000 customers and generated more than $10 million in revenue.** It was life-changing for us, and it worked because we focused on solving a specific problem for our audience.

People aren't looking for a business opportunity—they're looking for a solution. They want something that works, something that feels like a "money machine." With Dialing for Dollars, we gave them exactly that. Today, we've refined those techniques using modern tools like websites, voicemail, and automated systems. The core idea is still the same: create systems that pre-sell your product or service, bringing you highly qualified buyers who are ready to act.

## The secret is to focus on results, solve real problems, and show people exactly how they can achieve what they're looking for.

People are searching for solutions. More than anything, they want results. As Eugene Schwartz, one of the greatest marketers of all time, once said, "What people really want is a miracle." Schwartz made millions in the 1970s and 80s by understanding this simple truth.

The key, however, is presenting that miracle in a way people believe and trust. If it sounds too good to be true, they'll run from it. For example, when we launched our "Dialing for Dollars" program, we didn't just say, "Turn your answering machine into a money machine." Instead, we used Russ's headline that got straight to the point and sparked curiosity: "How do you get $843 every day receiving phone calls—and you never have to talk to a single person?"

**That headline worked because it promised a clear, specific result.** People want freedom from stress, financial security, and the ability to live life on their terms. They don't want the headaches of running a business or dealing with taxes and regulations. What they truly desire is a proven system—a way to achieve financial independence without the usual struggles.

## People love our systems because they offer genuine solutions to real problems.

The initial success of our company wasn't just because of the marketing. My wife, Eileen, did an incredible job running the company. Her practical, common-sense approach balanced my creative, sales-driven mindset. Together, we built a system that helped thousands of people find a path to financial freedom, generating millions of dollars.

33

Now, we want to share that same guidance and support with you. If you're ready to take the next step, fill out the form at the end of this book. You'll get access to our no-pressure sales system, along with 144 additional marketing secrets that can help you achieve your financial dreams.

We've been fortunate to learn from some of the best marketers in the world, including Russ Von Hoelscher, Dan Kennedy, and Eugene Schwartz. Now, it's your turn. Let us help you discover the tools, systems, and support to change your life forever—just like they helped us.

That's it for this small book. If you've enjoyed what you've read so far, let me tell you—this is just the tip of the iceberg. There's so much more to tell you.

What you've seen so far includes only five of the 144 little-known tips, tricks, and strategies that you'll find in my *No-Pressure Sales System* book.

This little book may be small, but it's powerful. It's pocket-sized—just 123 pages—so you can carry it with you wherever you go. Don't let the size fool you. The ideas packed inside are transformative.

Here's what I recommend: keep this book with you. Study a little bit each day. Keep it in your pocket, on your desk, or somewhere you can easily access it. Every time you pick it up, you'll uncover more of my best sales and marketing secrets. Over time, you'll learn exactly how to make massive amounts of money, transform your life, and master the sales process like a pro.

By the time you finish, you'll know more about selling and marketing than 99% of other salespeople—including most sales managers. You'll have my full collection of tips, tricks, and strategies to guide you every step of the way.

As an added bonus, when you order my *No-Pressure Sales System* book, you'll also receive a free 30-minute coaching session with me. This is a personal consultation designed to help you apply these methods and make more money using them.

You'll attend this session in a small, personalized online environment with just a handful of people. Some days it ends up being 1-on-1. But always small and informal. It's a chance for me to get to know you better, and for you to learn even more about these life-changing strategies.

During this session, we'll explore your goals, and look at whether you're a great fit for one of our coaching programs, like *No-Pressure Sales System Coaching*, *Direct Mail Mastery*, or our *Get More Customers Association.* Each one of these platforms offers a different level of Membership to help you take your results even further.

If you've liked what you've read, don't stop here. Fill out the form in the back of this book, send it in, and I'll rush you a copy of my *No-Pressure Sales System* book, along with your certificate for a free 30-minute coaching session.

Take the next step today. You'll be glad you did!

# Here are a Few of the Secrets You'll Discover in My No-Pressure Sales System Book.

I hope you've enjoyed getting just a handful of my top secrets in this small book. Let me send you my 123-page No-Pressure Sales System book and you'll get all 144 secrets in one easy to read book. **Here's just a few of the secrets in my book:**

* The power of **ethical manipulation** and why it matters. (pg. 5)

* Albert Einstein's greatest secret that makes you a ton of money! (pg. 5)

* **How a quiet and shy person can become sales superstar.** (pg. 6)

* The 500-year-old Shakespeare secret that makes you a fortune today. (pg. 8)

* Discover the 'magic sales bullet' and how to make it your secret weapon. (pg. 13)

* Dorothea Brande's secret from 1936 that's even more valuable today. (pg. 18)

* Cold calling sucks! Do this and you'll <u>never</u> make another cold call ever again. (pg. 23)

* How to let people chase you instead of you chasing them. (pg. 25)

* **An unusual secret from the 1950's that took one company from $18 million a year to $54 million a year—and that was 1950s money! It <u>works</u> <u>even</u> <u>better</u> <u>today</u>.** (pg. 33)

* The secret from a Nobel Prize winner that makes you big bucks! (pg. 40)

* The dumbest way to sell, and yet almost every salespeople does it. (pg. 45)

* Why great salespeople <u>love</u> objections, and so should you! (pg. 58)

* Zig Ziglar's ultimate sales success mantra for lasting joy and financial freedom. (pg. 58)

* The selling power of a **magical cure**. (pg. 60)

* Six unusual ways to sell <u>without</u> people knowing that they're being sold. (pg. 61)

* Are your sales sluggish? Do these four things. (pg. 63)

* The little-known secret of the greatest salespeople in the world. (pg. 64)

* How to make sales to the most skeptical buyers. (pg. 67)

* The 10 reasons why the right stories in your sales pitch will out-earn your competition. (pg. 68)

* **Buyers are liars!** Why 99% of the people who tell you they can't afford it or don't have the money are lying. (pg. 69)

* How to get **celebrity-like power** that draws people to you. (pg. 70)

* The awesome power of **indirect selling**. (pg. 72)

* Turn earning money into an exciting adventure you'll love! (pg. 75)

* The two most powerful sales and marketing principles that make you more money than all the others combined. (pg. 76)

* Six reasons why prospects don't buy right away. Hint: Not having the money is **not** one of these reasons! (pg. 80)

* How to get the best buyers to come to you **presold** and ready to buy! (pg. 89)

* One of the most powerful sales and marketing strategies you'll ever use is something your mother probably taught you. (pg. 89)

* The low-cost lead generation magnet that draws the best people to you. (pg. 89)

* A lesson from Hollywood that leads to long-term success. (pg. 94)

* The 23 unconscious emotional triggers that drive people to buy. (page 97)

* The quality of your life and business is **dependent** on this one thing. (pg. 99)

* **From $700,000 a year to delivering pizzas?** Absolutely! Here's the real story of one man's fall from a six-figure sales job to a low-paying, entry-level job. Let me tell you what went wrong in two key lessons. (pg. 102)

* How compete with dishonest salespeople and still make a lot of money. (pg. 104)

* Seven reasons why unreasonable people dominate the world! (pg. 107)

* How to get out of any sales slump. (pg. 108)

* **How to earn $18,000 in just one hour:** The incredible true story, supported by a simple, step-by-step formula. (pg. 109 to 110)

* Why there's no such thing as non-manipulative selling. (pg. 117 to 119)

* And so much more!

# Fill out the Form on the next page to get my No-Pressure Sales System book for just $12.95, shipped free.

# No-Pressure Sales System 144 Secrets ORDER FORM

**YES, T.J.!** I read your book and I'm ready to dive in deeper. I loved reading the six secrets presented in this book. I can't wait to get the bigger picture. I'm convinced that your secrets and strategies can help me achieve my goals and make more money. **I MUST KNOW MORE!** I understand that you've been helping people make money for over 36 years, and these secrets go all the way back to when you started your first business in the early 1980s. **Along with my No-Pressure Sales System book, please include a Voucher for 30 minutes of free coaching so you can help me use these secrets to make the most money in my business.**

**STEP #1:** Choose your option.

❏ Send your **No-Pressure Sales System book** with all 144 secrets, and the 30-minute Coaching Voucher for $12.95 (free s/h).

❏ *Say no more!* You've already convinced me. I know I need your help! Give me a **100-day Trial Membership** for just $100!

**STEP #2:** Provide your payment information.

Card Number _____ Expiration _____

Signature _____ Security Code _____

**STEP #3:** Give us your complete contact information.

Name _____ Address _____

City/State/Zip Code _____

Daytime Phone Number _____

Email Address _____

**INSTRUCTIONS:** Fill out this Form and **MAIL** or **FAX** it directly to us.

**MAIL to:** DRN • P.O. Box 198 • Goessel, KS 67053

**Or FAX to:** (316) 333-1941

*Submitting this Form constitutes an acceptance of the terms on the back.*

| For Internal Use Only: |
| --- |
| _____ |
| Referral ID Number |

www.ingramcontent.com/pod-product-compliance
Lightning Source LLC
Chambersburg PA
CBHW042123190326
41520CB00026B/7517